CONTENTS

BARRON'S

INCA LIFE

BY

DAVID DREW

Who Were the Incas?

SACRED LAKE

Lake Titicaca, 12,468 ft (3,800 meters) above sea level, was sacred to the Incas. Situated on the border between Peru and Bolivia, the god of creation, Viracocha, was said to have brought forth the sun, the moon, and the first humans from its waters. From here, the legendary founder of the Inca royal line, Manco Capac, traveled northwest to establish Cuzco as the Inca capital.

In the early 16th century the Incas controlled the greatest empire ever seen in the Americas. They came to prominence late and in A.D. 1400 they were little more than an inconspicuous highland tribe. But in less than a century, through war and diplomacy, they came to dominate some 10 million people within an empire, which in organization and scale rivaled that of the Romans. Their remote ancestors were Stone Age hunters who crossed from Asia to Alaska more than 12,000 years earlier. They moved south to populate what is now known as the Central Andes, running from Ecuador in the north, through modern-day Peru, and south to Bolivia and Chile. Here they slowly domesticated plants and animals to become settled farmers.

THE LOST CITY

The Incas were superb architects and stonemasons. The most beautiful and best preserved of all Inca cities, Machu Picchu was spread spectacularly across a mountain ridge and designed to achieve natural harmony with the surrounding landscape. Undiscovered by the Spaniards, it remained lost to the outside world until 1911.

LAND OF THE FOUR QUARTERS

The Incas' vast empire stretched more than 3,000 miles (4,800 km) from north to south. They called it *Tahuantinsuyu,* or "Land of the Four Quarters." At the heart lay Cuzco, which they thought of as the "navel" of the world. The empire included every kind of terrain, with deserts along the coast, the towering Andes mountains inland, and fringes of the Amazon jungle to the east.

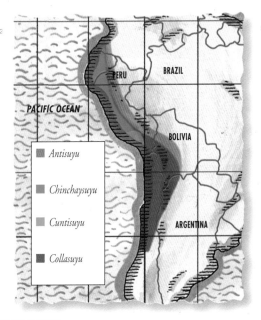

PERU
BRAZIL
PACIFIC OCEAN
BOLIVIA
ARGENTINA

▨ *Antisuyu*

▨ *Chinchaysuyu*

▨ *Cuntisuyu*

▨ *Collasuyu*

PORTRAIT OF THE PAST

This pottery "stirrup vessel" (so-called because of the stirrup-like shape of the handle and spout) depicts a ruler of the Moche, ancestors of the Incas who inhabited the north coast of Peru in the first centuries A.D. Such finely modeled pots give a vivid impression of the distinctive facial features of the early peoples of the Andes.

SACRED VALLEY

In the mountains just north of Cuzco lies the Urubamba valley. The Urubamba was a river as holy to the Incas as the Ganges is to Hindus. The temperate climate here was perfect for the cultivation of maize, the Incas' most prized crop.

COMMON WEALTH

The Incas respected the skills of others and the local traditions within their empire. The craftsmen of the north coast, for example, who produced this gold vessel, were the finest metalworkers in the Andes. When the Incas conquered the region in about A.D. 1470 their goldsmiths were taken to Cuzco to teach Inca apprentices.

Life for the Rich

*T*he Inca world was a rigidly ordered, hierarchical society. At the top was the emperor, known as the Sapa Inca or Unique Inca. He was considered a god by his people and retained absolute rule over his kingdom. The royal family controlled the priesthood and army and formed a royal council from four of the highest members of the nobility. Each one was in charge of a "suyu" (quarter) of the empire. The capital city of Cuzco, with its rich palaces and temples, was the domain of the royal and noble classes where they led lives of privilege and style, attended to by a retinue of servants. In Cuzco common people were kept at a considerable distance from the central precinct.

ROYAL CARRIAGE

The Incas had neither horses nor wheeled vehicles. When the ruler traveled he went in a wooden litter (single carriage) carried on the shoulders of porters. Here Topa Inca and his principal wife Mama Ocllo are seated beneath a canopy of feathers. Curtains protected them from the prying eyes of their subjects. This is one of nearly 200 drawings by Felipe Guaman Poma de Ayala, a man of native Inca blood who, at the turn of the 17th century, wrote a unique illustrated account of the everyday lives of his people.

INCA PRINCE

Some members of the royal family retained their status and privileges after the Spanish conquest. This detail from a late 17th century Cuzco painting shows a native prince wearing a mixture of Inca and Spanish dress. He has fine jewels added to his traditional headband. The lace of his sleeves, very European in style, is combined with a typical royal Inca geometric ornament across his waist.

DISPLAY OF POWER

In the main square of Cuzco and each provincial capital was a raised ceremonial platform called an *usnu* where the Inca ruler sat in state. Here he bears some of the most important symbols of his office, including circular plugs of gold in his ears and a braid of textile around his head, which supported the royal fringe of gold and woolen tassels, the equivalent of the crown of European kings.

NICE PLUMAGE

The royal family and the nobility, which included loyal allies around Cuzco and collaborators among the conquered, had special privileges. They alone were allowed to wear gold and silver and the finest quality cloth, and to sport a variety of headgear befitting their rank and place of origin. This woven crown of llama wool topped by macaw and egret feathers has been preserved by the desert sands of the Pacific coast.

DYNASTIC PORTRAIT GALLERY

These paintings in Spanish style are imaginary depictions of Inca rulers. Little is known about them apart from the seventh figure, known as Pachacuti. His name means "earthquake" or "revolution," and around A.D. 1440 he embarked on the first stage of Inca conquest. He was followed by Topa Inca Yupanqui, a great military leader who extended Inca power into Chile and Ecuador.

Life for the Poor

The majority of the Inca population was simple farmers and herdsmen who lived in villages and hamlets across the varied geography of the empire. However, few escaped the notice of the imperial administration. All Inca subjects were obliged to pay taxes—not in money, which did not exist under the Incas, but through labor. Men tilled royal, religious, and communal lands and were obliged to labor on construction projects, such as fortresses and roads. Women wove textiles, prepared food, and helped men on the land. Life was hard, but few went hungry. State storehouses were kept full of food, clothing, and other necessities to insure against famine and natural disasters.

OLD AGE

On average, most people would be fortunate to live beyond their 50s. Under the Inca system, when a man's physical ability to work in the fields declined, he qualified as a state pensioner. If his family could not care for him, he would be fed and clothed from the government storehouses.

GUARDING THE CROP

The maize crop was sown in September and nourished by the rains that came between November and January. In February, shelters were put up on the edges of fields and men and boys armed with slings protected the corn from predators until the harvest in May. Here, Guaman Poma (see page 4) depicts a suitably dressed figure warding off birds from the crops.

BY THE SEA

The dramatically contrasting natural environments within the empire determined much of the character of daily life. Those who lived on the coast had the rich resources of the sea at hand. Here a fisherman is seen paddling a canoe made from bundles of reeds.

TRAVAXA CHACRAMÃTAPISCO

6

IN THE MOUNTAINS

These modern houses, looking much like they would have in ancient times, are built of stone and mud-brick with thatched roofs. They stand at about 13,124 ft (4,000 meters) above sea level. At this height, the air is thin and it is very cold at night. Only potatoes and a few other root crops will grow at this altitude. The stone-walled enclosures are used to protect animals overnight.

COOPERATIVE SOCIETY

The most important social unit was a group of related families called an *ayllu*. Without horses and oxen all agricultural work was done by hand. The ayllu represented a pool of communal labor to ensure that each family's land was tended. Here, at the ceremonial start of the farming year in August, the earth is broken up with *chaqitacllas* (foot plows).

A SIMPLE HOUSE

Most Inca buildings were one-roomed, of rectangular form and arranged around an open courtyard where domestic activities would be carried out. This example is particularly well built, with finely-worked stones forming the right-angled corners. The thatched roof is attached to a wooden frame resting on top of the walls and tied to projecting stone pegs. There was no chimney, and smoke from the hearth simply rose up through the thatch.

Food & Drink

HOME OF THE POTATO

Inca farmers probably cultivated more than 200 different varieties of potato, which first appeared in domesticated form in the Andes 5,000 years ago. This ceramic plate contains *chuño*, a kind of freeze-dried potato that was kept in the imperial storehouses.

For most families meat was only eaten on special occasions. Their diet was based on potatoes, maize, and native grains, such as *quinoa*. Food was prepared in earthenware pots and cooked on a clay stove. The most common dishes were stews and soups, flavored with chili peppers and herbs. Ayllus often had lands widely spaced apart at different altitudes to grow varied produce—these were exchanged between families, ensuring a healthy, balanced diet. Potato fields and llama herds were found at high altitudes, maize and beans in the mid valleys, and foodstuffs, such as manioc, tomatoes, squash, and fruits, grew in the hotter regions of the lowlands. For drinking, every household prepared *chicha,* or beer, made from a number of plants and berries, but most commonly from fermented maize. It was kept cool in the house in large ceramic pots sunk halfway into the ground.

PROTEIN SOURCE

The Incas did not have cows, pigs, sheep, goats, chickens, or turkeys. The only meat eaten with any regularity was guinea pig. They ran around inside the house and were fed on plants and kitchen scraps. Llama was eaten occasionally, but along with the alpaca, it was considered too valuable for its fleece to be a regular part of the Inca diet.

DRINKING VESSEL

The powerful in society ate and drank from the finest pottery and precious metals, such as this silver drinking vessel. Fish, game, and rare fruits from the tropical forests of the east were brought to the imperial court in Cuzco by special teams of runners. In the capital, women who dedicated their lives to the sun god and the service of the ruler made the finest beer.

PRECIOUS CORN

Native to the Americas, maize is one of the most versatile and nutritious of all plant foods. In ancient times it was toasted, boiled, eaten on the cob, turned into the original popcorn, or ground into flour and steamed to produce dough cakes. This maize plant, cast in silver, is one of the rare and legendary treasures of the Incas.

TERRACED LANDSCAPE

The best way to cultivate the steep hillsides effectively was to build agricultural terraces. Great engineering skill and large workforces transformed vast areas of the Andean landscape for crops. Constructed with stone retaining walls, they were irrigated by canals which brought water from rivers and springs.

BEARING A BURDEN

This ceramic model shows a man carrying a typical Inca storage jar called an *urpu* or *aryballus*. Such containers held shelled maize or chicha and the small mug in front of him may have been for drinking the contents of the jar.

Pastimes

The Inca work ethic was strong, but it would be wrong to think that Andean people did not make time to enjoy themselves. Little is known about popular games played in the home. Guaman Poma and Spanish authors who wrote accounts of Inca society soon after the conquest report on athletic contests among the sons of the nobility. Games of chance and with dice are briefly mentioned, but with little explanation of the rules. Hunting was the great sport of Inca rulers—like their counterparts in medieval Europe, they established large game reserves where the penalty was death for poachers of deer or guanaco, a wild relative of the llama. Most ordinary folk looked forward to those precious times in the agricultural year when respite was offered from the drudgery of work on the land. Then communities would come together for music, dance, eating, and drinking, which would continue for many days.

IMPENETRABLE SPIRIT WORLD

Religious rituals were constant and much free time was devoted to the making of ceremonial artifacts, such as this striking human mask from the north coast of Peru. It is thought to have been an ornament from a headdress.

FI ESTAS DE LOS ANDISVIOS
CAIACAIAVARMIAVCA

JUNGLE RHYTHM

Each part of the empire had its own traditions of music and dance. Here Guaman Poma illustrates what he says was the typical dance of the people known as the *Antis,* who came from the jungle regions to the east of Cuzco.

FESTIVAL OF THE SUN

Still performed in Cuzco, the Festival of the Sun or *Inti Raymi* (*Inti* meaning sun), commemorated the maize harvest at the June solstice. It was one of the principal events in the religious calendar. The Inca ruler led thanksgiving for the crops of the past year and offered prayers and sacrifices to ensure the sun's continued strength in the months to come.

THE OLD POTTER

Today, as in ancient times, many ordinary farmers possess great talent as part-time craftsmen. This elderly villager still makes pots for household use and like his ancient ancestors, he builds them from coils of clay. Spread out in front of him are some of the simple tools that he employs, mostly made of llama bone.

BEER GOBLET

Impressive wooden goblets, like this in the form of a human head, would normally be made in pairs for elaborate toasting. Feasts and ritual drinking were serious business and the state sponsorship of local festivals was essential to keep everyone happy.

MUSIC

Inca music involved a combination of wind and percussion instruments. String instruments only appeared after the Spanish conquest. In the wind section they used simple flutes called *qenas* and pan pipes, both of which are still played today. There were pottery trumpets, horns made from conch shells, and a great variety of drums.

Fashion

The Andes is the home of one of the world's most astonishing and enduring weaving traditions. The main vehicle for personal display was finely woven and brilliantly colored cloth. We know that the Inca ruling classes kept themselves scrupulously groomed. The royal family bathed frequently in baths lined with cut stone, through which water was sometimes piped from hot springs. Most men, it seems, wore their hair trimmed in a fringe in the front and long in the back. Women rarely cut their lustrous dark hair—it was parted down the middle and often twisted into fine plaits. The same style of garment was worn by royalty and peasants alike but was distinguished by the quality of the cloth. There is little record of the use of makeup among Inca women, though warriors and priests regularly painted their faces and limbs.

TINY FIGURE

This miniature male figure was originally wrapped in textiles. The most striking features are the pierced and distended earlobes, caused by the weight of the large metal earplugs that were commonly worn by noblemen. Thus the Spaniards called Incas of rank *orejones* (big ears).

BAG OF GOLD

Small bags or pouches were carried by both women and men. The most ostentatious weavings might be sewn with feathers and threaded with gold and silver, or have small plates of precious metals attached.

MODERN DRESS

Today a person's home village can be identified by the patterns of the textiles he or she wears. Yet forms of clothing have changed. Women's dresses and men's tunics have not been worn since the end of the 18th century when traditional clothing was banned, as it was seen as inciting rebellion.

LADY'S CHAMBER

The "Coya" (Inca Queen) is tended to by her servants. Women wore a long, sleeveless one-piece dress and a mantle around the shoulders, often used by common folk for carrying children or produce. Like the male tunic, the queen's dress is also ornamented with *tocapus*.

SHEEP OF THE ANDES

The soft, thick fleece of the alpaca, cousin of the llama, was ideal for clothing. An even finer wool, reserved for the elite in society, was that of the vicuña. The most prestigious textiles of all were made by women known as *acllas*, who dedicated their lives to weaving, the preparation of food, and making chicha for the imperial society and the gods.

ROYAL TUNIC

Men wore tunics, such as this one made from a mixture of cotton and alpaca fiber. Natural dyes like cochineal and indigo produced the rich colors. The individual geometric designs in rectangular compartments across the waist were called tocapus. They would have indicated the origins and status of the wearer, who, given the magnificent quality of the tunic, may have been a member of the royal family.

Art & Architecture

The Incas are famed for their skills in weaving and metalwork. But it was the working of stone, both as sculpture and in architecture, which appealed to them more than any other form of artistic expression and in which they truly excelled. Their temples, palaces, and fortresses display astonishing techniques of stonemasonry. In some buildings they used crisply cut rectangular blocks laid in courses like rows of sugar lumps. In others, massive irregularly-shaped stones were fitted perfectly together without the use of mortar. Inca architecture left the Spaniards awestruck and their achievements still astonish visitors today.

MASTER CRAFTSMEN

The skilled Inca stonemason would tirelessly chip away at each block with a hammer of another harder stone until the required shape was achieved for it to fit alongside its neighbor. Such is the quality of Inca stonework that even today scholars do not fully understand all the techniques used, nor the methods by which they detached and transported enormous blocks of stone from the quarries.

SACRED ROCK

Inca sculptors would carve steps, platforms, and abstract shapes out of large boulders and outcrops, transforming features of their homeland into sacred places for religious ritual.

IMPERIAL CAPITAL

European illustrations show how impressed the Spanish were by the Inca architecture in the city. There were four major gateways with roads leading toward each of the quarters of Tahuantinsuyu. At the very heart of the city was an enormous plaza, used for festivals and public performances, where the usnu, or ceremonial platform, was positioned.

CARVED STONE DISH

Inca sculptors also created small worked and polished items such as this stone mortar with a relief design of writhing snakes. Even a more modest, useful object such as this has an impressive quality.

SACSAHUAMAN

The most remarkable example of the sheer scale of Inca architecture is to be found at Sacsahuaman, on a hill directly overlooking Cuzco. The walls are made up of blocks weighing as much as 220,400 lbs (100 tons). Indeed, it is said that Cuzco was laid out in the form of a puma. The great architectural projects of the Incas required enormous numbers of workers, drafted to provide their labor tax to the state. It is thought that some 30,000 men must have worked on Sacsahuaman over a 20–30 year period. It was a fortress and place of refuge, but also a holy place, with temples within its walls.

Health & Medicine

The Incas were physically well adapted to their demanding environment, with broad shoulders and strong legs to deal with the transport of heavy goods up and down the mountains. Deep chests with extra lung capacity compensated for the lack of oxygen. To help counteract altitude sickness, hunger, and fatigue they chewed the mildly narcotic leaves of the coca bush, which grows on the fringes of the jungle. Many ailments were treated with herbal remedies—potions and infusions were handed down from one local curer to another. From villages northeast of Lake Titicaca came a famous group of wandering healers called the "Collahuayas," who would be summoned to Cuzco to treat the royal family. Inca medical knowledge, in the more scientific sense of the word, was limited. As in many ancient and traditional societies, physical illness was often considered to reflect a spiritual sickness, or a problem in the relationship between humans and the gods.

FOREIGN DISEASES

European diseases, such as smallpox, measles, and even influenza, were unknown in the Americas before the arrival of the Spaniards. The Incas had no immunity to these illnesses and died in appallingly large numbers.

PLANT MEDICINE

Some plants had very specific uses. The leaves of the chillca plant, for example, when heated and applied to the skin, were said to relieve rheumatism. Sarsaparilla was used to cure painful sores. The molle tree had multiple benefits; its red berries were used to make beer, the bark was boiled and applied to wounds to speed healing, and the twigs were used as a toothbrush.

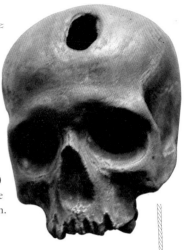

BRAIN SURGERY

The Incas were famous for a crude but effective surgical technique known as trepanation: the drilling or cutting of a hole in the skull, probably with a copper knife. This may have been done to release pressure on the brain from battle injuries inflicted by stone clubs. Patients were anesthetized with concoctions made from jungle plants. Even chicha beer was used as a method of relieving pain. Many evidently survived, since in 50 percent of the skulls analyzed there is evidence that the hole had partly closed up again after the operation.

CARE OF THE SICK

In his writings, Guaman Poma emphasized the care given to the sick and elderly during Inca times. Here, an old man lying on the floor on a mat (the Incas had little furniture) is fed a wholesome bowl of broth.

SHAMANS & WITCH DOCTORS

A large number of deities or supernatural forces inhabiting mountaintops, caves, or other features of the landscape were thought to affect the well-being of ordinary people. Ritual offerings, such as the burning of coca leaves or the sacrifice of an animal, would be made to placate them and restore a patient to health. This was led by a shaman or witch doctor who was thought capable of turning himself into powerful creatures able to communicate with the spirits.

EVIDENCE OF DISEASE

Some strikingly realistic pots depicted deformities and diseases, some of them unique to the Americas before the invasion of the Spanish. These included leishmaniasis with symptoms resembling leprosy and syphilis, which is shown here.

SESTA CALLE
CORO·TASQVE

YOUNG HERDSMAN

Accounts of everyday
farming life describe the
typical activities of each age
group. This boy of 12
was not yet strong enough
to join his father in tilling
the fields. Instead, his
duties involved tending
animals, collecting firewood
or grasses for thatching
the house, and keeping
pests away from the fields.

Family Life

 arming families were organized into groups of 100 taxpayers, each under the charge of a local *curaca,* or administrator. One of his duties was to perform marriages. Girls were prepared for marriage at 16; for boys it was between 18 and 25. Both were obliged to take partners from within their own ayllu and once betrothed they would be assigned lands by the community. In Cuzco there were special schools to teach the sons of the nobility the responsibilities of power. In the countryside there were no schools, so age-old skills were passed on in the fields and the home. Occasionally, an outstandingly clever or beautiful child might be chosen to go to Cuzco to serve the emperor. Some girls were selected as acllas—they lived in convents, away from public gaze, and dedicated their lives to religion, weaving, and the state. In the village it was a matter of great family pride to be chosen.

AMOROUS POT

A ceramic vessel made
by the Nazca people of
the southern coast of
Peru shows a couple
embracing. The ancient
potters of the Andes
never used glazes.
Instead, a wide
range of pigments
was used and the
surface of a pot
was burnished
to achieve the
colorful polished
effect seen here.

STERN UPBRINGING

Healthy children were a great blessing in a society where infant mortality was high and a family's wealth was measured in terms of the labor it could muster. However, there was little pampering of infants, who had a spartan upbringing. They were washed in cold water, exposed in their cradles to frosty nights and damp mornings, and shown few signs of affection. Girls helped their mothers with younger children and learned household tasks, such as cooking and weaving.

A LAZY COUPLE

A couple enjoys a nap, a rare event when the whole family normally lived in one room and shared the same bed. Possessions and food were kept in clay pots, in the attic or hung on pegs on the walls.

OFFERINGS TO THE GODS

In recent years tiny gold or silver figures such as this, dressed in woven mantles, have been found buried on mountaintops with the frozen remains of children. These children, chosen for their beauty and other special qualities, were sacrificed with great honor as offerings to the gods. It was a ritual performed very rarely to give strength and bring prosperity to the ruler and the empire as a whole.

MARRIAGE ALLIANCE

Very soon after the conquest, Spaniards began to take Inca wives, in the absence of European women. Thus appeared the first *mestizos,* or children of mixed blood. The groom depicted here is Martín García de Loyola, the Spaniard who in 1572 captured the last Inca ruler, Tupac Amaru, who was executed soon afterward. The bride is Tupac Amaru's niece, given the Spanish name Doña Beatriz. The marriage was viewed as deeply symbolic, anticipating harmony between the races, which in reality never came.

War & Weaponry

Although they preferred to enlarge their empire by diplomatic means, Inca power undoubtedly grew through aggressive wars. Their conquests began in the highlands and around Lake Titicaca before Inca armies descended on the Pacific coast. By the time of Topa Inca's death in 1493, the empire had almost reached its zenith. Inca tactics and weaponry were unsophisticated but effective. Battles would begin with volleys of sling stones, then hand-to-hand combat with spears and fearsome maces or clubs. They also employed a kind of battle-ax of copper or a soft bronze, which was developed just before the Spanish conquest.

FORTRESSES

The period before the Incas was one of conflict in the Cuzco region. Tribes built their towns and villages on hilltops as a means of defense. The initial wars of Pachacuti involved the besieging and storming of fortresses such as the one depicted here.

JUNGLE WARRIOR

This detail from a wooden kero shows a warrior from the tropical forests wearing a typical feather headdress. Renowned for their skills with the bow and arrow, the jungle tribes were enlisted as mercenaries by the Incas.

WARRIOR PREPARING FOR BATTLE

Behind this squatting warrior is a stone mace, and next to it a spear-thrower and darts. He is chewing coca leaves, kept in a bag in front of him, to compose himself for battle. The long stick contains lime, which helps to release the stimulant from the leaves.

SACSAHUAMAN

Looming above the city of Cuzco, Sacsahuaman had triple-terraced ramparts whose giant zig-zags meant that an approaching attacker would always be exposed on one flank. This enormous fortified complex was the site of bitterly contested battles at the time of the Spanish conquest.

PACHACUTI

The first great imperial ruler is seen here, with shield and club in his left hand and wielding a sling in his right. Like all Inca people he wears simple leather sandals, but his headdress and bands of tocapus he bears upon his tunic would have revealed who he was.

CATAPULTING STONES

This pottery vessel shows a warrior holding a sling, from which a stone the size of an egg or small apple would be catapulted at tremendous speed toward the enemy. This warrior keeps a second sling in reserve by using it as a headband.

Crime & Punishment

DREADFUL DUNGEON

A story is told of an underground chamber in Cuzco filled with snakes, pumas, jaguars, and other ferocious creatures. Those convicted of treason or particularly insulting behavior toward the Inca ruler were cast in here to be devoured. In the highly unlikely event that a person survived for more than three days, he would be pulled out and pardoned.

At the time of the conquest the Spanish noted what law-abiding citizens the Incas were and the natural respect they showed for authority. This reflected the nature of the Inca state system, which demanded total submission to its will and exerted control over almost every aspect of commoners' lives. Each suyu (quarter) was divided into provinces that were overseen by a hierarchy of local administrators. These men fixed the tax obligations of every community, encouraged improvements in the local economy, and administered Inca laws. The Inca legal system decreed that no one should be idle and that central government and its officials and the worship of the sun should be respected at all times. Few transgressed, willing to exchange what we would regard as individual freedom for the undoubted peace, security, and relative well-being that Inca rule brought. Those who did disobey could expect severe retribution, though no more brutal than the level of punishment inflicted by European rulers on their subjects.

COMMUNITY COUNCIL

Village lands did not belong to the individual but to the local ayllu. The personal use of land was reviewed annually by the ayllu and much the same system applies in Peru today. Minor laws were also established and policed at the local level.

BOUND PRISONER

This modeled pot depicts the Andean equivalent of the stocks in colonial America. A prisoner is tied to a wooden frame in what appears to be a form of public humiliation. Condemned criminals were staked out in the desert to be eaten alive by vultures.

MACHU PICCHU PRISONS

Hiram Bingham, the American explorer who revealed the existence of Machu Picchu to the outside world in 1911, called one section of buildings the "prison group." It includes subterranean rooms and natural caves, which may have served as dungeons. As a rule, physical punishment was preferred over imprisonment.

SACRIFICIAL BLOOD

In Inca times the practice of human sacrifice was rare. But this was not so among earlier peoples. Moche pottery and mural painting present a repeated theme where bound prisoners have their throats cut and the blood is collected in special goblets carried by individuals in a procession.

DEADLY TUMBLE

The death sentence was often passed for theft and adultery, as well as for murder. Execution could be by stoning, being clubbed to death, or by being thrown over a precipice. Alternatively, offenders were hanged from a cliff by the hair until they fell to their deaths.

Transport & Technology

The Incas are often compared to the Romans because of their energy and effectiveness as soldiers, engineers, and administrators. They developed an enormous network of roads, along which were garrisons, way stops called *tambos* for official travelers, and a vast infrastructure of storage facilities. Inca armies and bureaucrats hurried down these highways on foot accompanied by herds of load-bearing llamas. When a new province was added to the empire, capitals were built in Inca style and administrators were installed to carry out surveys of the economic potential of the region. The highland tongue "Quechua" was established as the language of imperial government. However, the Incas had no written language. Instead, the tool of the official was the *quipu*, a system of knotted and colored cords used to record statistical information.

KNOTTED CODE

The quipu was a horizontal piece of cord from which hung vertical strings of different colors, knotted at intervals. Many quipus survive, but although the Incas are known to have followed a decimal system of counting, the exact way in which they worked and any additional information that they stored is not known.

SUSPENSION BRIDGE

Fragile looking but extremely strong bridges made of braided rope were used to span rivers and ravines. They were anchored at each end on stone platforms. They did not need to be very broad, since the only traffic was humans and slim, sure-footed llamas.

THE ROAD SYSTEM

At its height the empire contained more than 15,625 miles (25,000 km) of roads, including a major route through the highlands and another that ran parallel along the coast. These two main arteries were linked by numerous other highways and local networks.

SPECIAL DELIVERY

Stationed along the highways at regular intervals were relays of runners called *chasquis,* who would race off with messages, in verbal or quipu form, to the next post a few miles down the road. Handed on from runner to runner, it would take no more than two days for important news to arrive in Cuzco from the coast. Here a chasqui blows a conch shell trumpet to announce his arrival.

ROAD HAULAGE

Llamas and alpacas were the only animal carriers that the Incas possessed. They are still used in Peru and Bolivia today. They live on the high grasslands, and can carry loads of 88–110 pounds (40–50 kg), and cover up to 12.5 miles (20 km) a day.

HIGHWAY OF THE SUN

Inca roads were built to last and many can still be traced today. Along the desert coast only a single wall or embankment may have marked their route, but in other places, such as the approach to mountain passes, they become broad, paved highways, stepped in the steeper sections.

Religion

HUACAS

Sacred places or objects were known as *huacas*. Man-made artifacts could be huacas but the most powerful of all were mountains, springs, caves, or other features of the natural world, which were thought to possess magical powers. Here a priest prepares to sacrifice a black llama at the site of a local huaca.

*T*he state religion involved worship of the sun (inti). The emperor was perceived as the embodiment of the sun's life-giving power on earth. His wife, the coya, was associated with the moon. At the precise center of Cuzco stood the Temple of the Sun, the most holy place in the empire. Inside there were also images of Viracocha, Venus, Rainbow, Thunder, and other ancient deities. There were ceremonies all year round in the city, with major sun festivals in June and December. These were duplicated on a smaller scale in the outposts of the empire. Although they were eager to build a unified kingdom, the Inca authorities were very careful to maintain the independent cultural traditions of conquered peoples. This was one of the secrets of their success as empire builders. Local temples and objects of worship that had flourished for centuries were largely left alone, though the holiest images of foreign peoples might be brought to the capital.

ROYAL MUMMIES

After the death of an Inca ruler, the body was embalmed and then remained in his palace to be worshipped as an ancestral god. Royal mummies were regularly paraded around Cuzco and even sat in on the councils of their descendants.

VISITING THE DEAD

Veneration of the dead was universal. People visited tombs and regularly consulted their ancestors, who were thought to still have an influence on the affairs of the living. The people from around Lake Titicaca,

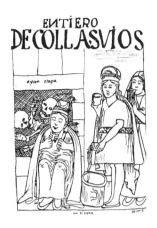

depicted here, laid their dead to rest in tall, finely constructed stone burial towers.

SOLAR TEMPLE

At the end of this street in Machu Picchu, perched on a large rock, stands a building known as the Torreon. It has an unusual rounded form, like the Coricancha in Cuzco, and is one of the finest examples of Inca masonry surviving today. It may have been the city's sun temple; the window seen here may have been used to take sightings of the solstice sunrise.

MOUNTAIN WORSHIP

This sculpted granite outcrop stands in the center of Machu Picchu at the very highest point of the city. For many years it has been known as the Intihuatana or "place where the sun is tied" in the belief that it had an astronomical purpose and acted as a kind of sundial. More recently, some have suggested that it is connected with the worship of sacred mountains and may indeed represent a mountain peak in abstract form. Machu Picchu was surrounded by imposing mountains, among which the Incas lived. These were the most holy and powerful of all natural phenomena and they were seen as the source of rain and thus of life itself.

ENCLOSURE OF GOLD

The Temple of the Sun in Cuzco was called the *Coricancha* or *Golden Enclosure*. The walls were covered with sheets of gold and an enormous golden image of the sun was housed here, along with countless other treasures. Today all that remains is some of the temple's exquisite stonework, seen here beneath the later Spanish church.

The Fall of the Incas

In 1532 Francisco Pizarro and 260 Spanish adventurers landed on the north coast of Peru. They headed inland and met with the Inca ruler Atahualpa, who was tricked and held hostage. A vast ransom in gold and silver was collected, enough to fill a small room almost to the ceiling. The treasure was melted down and sent back to Spain. The Spaniards, however, stayed. They murdered Atahualpa and traveled south to Cuzco in the company of his half-brother Manco, whom Pizarro hoped to control as a puppet ruler. An uneasy peace ensued for two years, but Spanish looting and the destruction of temples and palaces intensified as thousands more Europeans arrived to join in the gold rush. In 1536, realizing at last that the empire was on the verge of destruction, Manco fled from Cuzco, assembled Inca forces, and laid siege to the city. He very nearly triumphed, but relief for the Spaniards came just in time. Manco escaped to the jungle and never saw Cuzco again.

THE END OF THE INCAS

In 1572, the Spanish successfully invaded Vilcabamba and the last of the Inca royal line, Tupac Amaru, was led in chains to his execution in Cuzco. Also seized was the mummy of his father, Manco, and a famous golden image of the sun.

VILCABAMBA EXILE

In the remote jungle-clad valleys of Vilcabamba, northwest of Machu Picchu, Manco Inca, his two sons, and their followers maintained a tiny Inca nation in exile for nearly 40 years. From here they mounted guerrilla raids on the Spanish. Remnants of the last Inca capital still lie buried deep in the jungle.

THE CAPTURE OF ATAHUALPA

The provincial town of Cajamarca saw the most dramatic scene in the fall of the Inca empire. Atahualpa came to the town with thousands of unarmed warriors to negotiate with the Spanish. However, they cut down his escort and captured the Inca leader. Once their semi-divine absolute ruler was in Spanish hands, the empire was paralyzed.

DESTRUCTION OF IDOLS

Hard on the heels of the military defeat of the Incas came the great campaign of religious conversion, the "spiritual conquest." Sacred images, tombs, mummies—every manifestation of idolatrous practice—was rooted out and destroyed.

BURIED TREASURE

This tiny golden llama provides a reminder of the wealth of the Inca empire. It has been estimated that Atahualpa's ransom alone may have been worth $50 million in today's terms.

PIZARRO & ALMAGRO

Equally ruthless and driven by greed, the two leaders of the Spanish conquest fought over the division of the spoils. Diego de Almagro was murdered by Pizarro's men in 1538, and in 1541 Pizarro himself was cut down by Almagro's followers in his palace in Lima.

Legacy of the Past

The effects of the Spanish conquest were devastating. By the end of the 16th century epidemic disease had reduced the native population from around ten million to less than one million. Towns and villages were deserted, storehouses that had once been full of food and clothing lay empty. Yet over the centuries, facing defeat, subjection, and forced labor in mines and on plantations, the people of the Andes showed astonishing resilience. Today the number of those who speak Quechua, the Inca language, is much as it was in the days of the empire. Isolation has been the key to the survival of Andean traditions. The Spaniards established Lima, on the Pacific coast, as their capital city and link with the home country. This created two very separate worlds—a colonial society centered on Lima that looked outward to Europe and an indigenous way of life that survived much as before in the mountainous interior.

SOLID AS A ROCK

Much of Cuzco was destroyed and its ancient buildings dismantled to build Spanish churches and houses. But throughout the centre of the city, imposing sections of Inca wall can be seen supporting later Colonial constructions. As the flimsier Spanish edifices have been toppled by time and earthquake these have remained unmoved.

CONSTANT THREAD

The people of the Andes possess the oldest unbroken weaving tradition anywhere in the world. The first simple fabrics were produced on the Peruvian coast 5,000 years ago. Today, cheap commercially produced cloth is seen in every home. But in traditional farming communities, women still take great pride in making ponchos, shawls, and other clothes for their family, using timeless techniques.

PAST & FUTURE

There are strong continuities between ancient times and the present day, but the people of the Andes do not live in a time warp. The city of Cuzco is a monument to the Incas, but now it is also a regional capital and a center for modern industry, agriculture, and tourism. In fact it is the money from foreign visitors who come here fascinated by the Inca past which provides income for many inhabitants. The people of the Andes have learned much about their own history and have forged a new identity as modern heirs of the Incas.

BRING & BUY

The marketplace in the highland towns is where traditional people from farming communities gather to sell or exchange their goods. They sell crafts, pottery, weavings, and agricultural products, such as maize and potatoes.

PUTTING THE PAST BACK TO WORK

Due to the scale of depopulation after the conquest, most of the great systems of agricultural terraces and irrigation canals, which had produced bumper crops in Inca times, were abandoned and have lain idle ever since. Today, rural populations are on the increase in many areas, so farmers are beginning to restore and revitalize the unused land of their ancestors to provide a better future for their children.

MANCO CAPAC

Manco Capac, the mythical founder of the Incas, has been commemorated with this magnificent statue. It is situated between the old town and the new airport in Cuzco.

DID YOU KNOW?

That the word "guano" means dung?
It refers to the enormous deposits of bird droppings that accumulated on the islands off the Peruvian coast. It was one of the best fertilizers in the world until the supply was exhausted in the 19th century.

Which famous bear traveled from Peru to England?
Paddington Bear; he came by boat and arrived in Paddington Station to find the Brown family. His favorite snack was marmalade sandwiches.

PRONUNCIATION
This is how to say the names of the most popular Inca words and rulers:

COMMON WORDS

Aclla (chosen women of the emperor, also known as "Virgins of the Sun")
pronounced **Ak-lya**

Ayllu (group of related families or community)
pronounced **Eye-lyu**

Chaquitaclla (Andean foot plow or digging stick)
pronounced **Cha-key-tack-lya**

Chicha (beer, commonly made from maize)
pronounced **Chee-Cha**

Coya (name given to the principal wife of the ruler, since he often had several)
pronounced **Koy-Ya**

Chuño (freeze-dried potatoes)
pronounced **Chew-nyo**

Huaca (a holy place, object, or shrine)
pronounced **Wa-Ka**

Inti (the sun)
pronounced **Een-Tee**

Quipu (knotted strings used to record information)
pronounced **Key-Poo**

Suyu (a quarter or division of the Inca empire)
pronounced **Sue-Yoo**

Usnu (a platform or throne of the emperor situated in the main square)
pronounced **Oosh-Noo**

INCA RULERS

Pachacuti (1438–1471)
pronounced **Pat-char-coo-tee**

Topa Inca (1471–1493)
pronounced **Toe-pa-inker**

Huayna Capac (1493–1527)
pronounced **Why-ner-kap-ak**

Atahualpa (1532–1533)
pronounced **Ater-wal-per**

Manco (1533–1545)
pronounced **Man-ko**

Tupac Amaru (1571–1572)
pronounced **Too-pack-amar-roo**

First edition for the United States, its territories and dependencies, Canada, and the Philippine Republic, published 2000 by Barron's Educational Series, Inc.

Original edition copyright © 2000 by ticktock Publishing Ltd. U.S. edition copyright © 2000 by Barron's Educational Series, Inc.
All inquiries should be addressed to: Barron's Educational Series, Inc., 250 Wireless Boulevard, Hauppauge, New York 11788
http://www.barronseduc.com
Library of Congress Catalog Card No. 99-68837   International Standard Book No. 0-7641-1069-1   Printed in Spain
9 8 7 6 5 4 3 2 1

Picture Credits:
t=top, b=bottom, c=center, l=left, r=right, OFC=outside front cover, IFC=inside front cover, IBC=inside back cover, OBC=outside back cover

AKG (London): 6tl, 15tl, 16/17c, 16tl, 21br & OBCtr, 23bl, 24bc, 27br, 29cr, OBCtl & OBCbc. Ancient Art & Architecture Collection: 2/3c & OBCcr, 3br, 3tr, 9c, 13tl, 18tl, 23tl, 25br, 26tl, 26bl. Archivo Fotográfico: 5br. Corbis: 27bl. David Drew: 4tl, 5tr, 7t, 11tr, 10bl, 13bl, 12b, 14tl, 16bl, 17tc, 19cr, 18bl, 21b, 20tl, 22tl, 22bl, 23cr, 25tr, 28bl, 28tl, 31cl. e. t. archive: 4br, 7br, 8tl, 17br, 19bc, 19tl, 20bl, 28/29c, OFC(main pic) & OFCbr. Image Select: 17tr, 29tl. Oxford Scientific Films: 8bl, 12tr & IFC. Pictor: 2tl, 2bl, 3cr, 11tl, 14/15, 30bl, 31tl, 31cr & OFCcr. Picture Colour Library: 10/11c, 31b. Werner Forman Archive: 4/5c, 6br, 6bl, 7bl, 8/9c, 9tr, 9br, 10tl, 11br, 12tl, 13r, 15tr, 18/19bc, 21t, 20br, 23br, 24l, 24/25c, 27tl, 27tr, 30tl, 32c.

INDEX